BRAIN

GRAMMAR IN THE NATIONAL CURRICULUM FOR AGE 7 - 9

Patricia and Steve Harrison

CONTENTS

Notes

The **"English for ages 5 to 16"** proposals published in June 1989 contained the following statement.

"We do not propose to specify lists of terms and concepts which should be taught ... It is the responsibility of teachers themselves to decide on and introduce terms as they become necessary ..." Para 5.30.

The paragraph goes on however to list 'terms' which 'are likely to be necessary' and ends each section with an *etc.*

In making our selection for this book we have attempted to provide breadth across the themes and depth in those areas which we feel warrant it. The first two pages are designed to assist teachers in linking the material in this book to their recording procedures for the National Curriculum.

It is worth remembering (and a convenient defence on occasions!) that grammar is not an exact science. As David Crystal reminds us in **'Rediscover Grammar'**:

"There are always exceptions to rules, and sometimes there are so many exceptions that it is awkward deciding what the rule should be."

So when you encounter difficulties console yourself knowing you are engaged in a creative process!

© 1991 Folens Limited, on behalf of the authors.

ISBN 1 85276048-6

First published 1990 by Folens Limited
Albert House, Apex Business Centre, Boscombe Road, Dunstable LU5 4RL

Covers by Hybert Design and Type
Illustration by Elaine Baker and Dandi Palmer
Cover photograph by Salem Krieger

NATIONAL CURRICULUM: ENGLISH for Key Stage 2

ATTAINMENT TARGET 3
WRITING (para 17.34)

A growing ability to construct and convey meaning in written language matching style to audience and purpose.

LEVEL	DESCRIPTION (GRAMMAR ASPECTS ONLY)
2	i) Produce, independently, pieces of writing using complete sentences, some of them demarcated with capital letters and full stops or question marks.
3	i) Produce, independently, pieces of writing using complete sentences, mainly demarcated with capital letters and full stops or question marks.
4	i) Produce pieces of writing in which there is a rudimentary attempt to present simple subject matter in a structured way... in which sentence punctuation (capital letters, full stops, question marks and exclamation marks) is generally accurately used; and in which there is some evidence of an ability to set out and punctuate any direct speech in a way that makes meaning clear to the reader.

Ref in Report	PROPOSED ASPECTS OF ENGLISH	RELEVANT SHEETS IN GRAMMAR AND THE NATIONAL CURRICULUM
5.30	LANGUAGE FORMS the sentence grammar of English	LOWER JUNIORS AGE 7 - 9
"	Adjectives	5 - 10
"	Singular and plural	47 - 48
"	Gender	43 - 44
" 17.40	Tenses	45 - 46
"	Nouns	11 - 13
"	Pronouns	14 - 15
5.30 17.41	Capital letters	17 - 20, 22 - 25
"	Full stops	21 - 25
"	Question marks	34 - 37
"	Exclamation marks	40 - 41
5.30 17.43	Inverted commas	26 - 31
"	Apostrophes	38 - 39

ATTAINMENT TARGET 3: WRITING GRAMMAR

CLASS RECORD Names	LEVEL 2					LEVEL 3					LEVEL 4				
			Some use of					Mainly use				Punctuate accurately with			
	Use complete sentences	Work independently	Capital Letters	Full Stops	Question Marks	Use complete sentences	Work independently	Capital Letters	Full Stops	Question Marks	Exclamation Marks	Full Stops	Capital Letters	Question Marks	Evidence of the use of speech marks

◻ covered   achieved satisfactorily

ADJECTIVES: NOUNS: PRONOUNS

Basic Definitions

Adjective
Describes a noun or *qualifies* a noun.

Noun
A *naming* word; can refer to a place, a person, a thing etc.

Pronoun
A word which *stands for* (i.e. substituting or replacing) a noun.

Individual Masters

Adjectives

Sheet 5 Each picture presents a different image of Mark Sterling. There are no definitive correct answers and it will be valuable to draw out the fact that the different adjectives can be equally appropriate. As adjectives describe or qualify nouns you may wish to emphasise that the word written describes Mark each time.

Sheet 6 Here is the process reversed. The adjective is provided and the child interprets the word through the drawing.

Sheet 7 The use of the single word adjective is taken a step further by the second task. Adjectives should now be included in sentences and their proximity to nouns can be explored.

Sheets 8-9 These sheets require some careful, specific writing. The adjectives used will need to be precise enough to allow the partner to distinguish between the options.

Sheet 10 Here the appropriateness of certain adjectives can be discussed.

Nouns

Sheet 11 The task involves naming elements from the picture. The key idea to draw out is that nouns cover a wide category of things, people and places.

Sheet 12 Nouns are divided here into Common and Proper. The link is established between the capital letter and Proper nouns.

Sheet 13 Some pupils will spot that some of the words at the top of the page begin with a capital letter and they may categorise them accordingly. You may wish to add to the list verbally to check whether the categorisation is based on an understanding of Proper/Common.

Pronouns

Sheet 14 A basic substitution exercise where the pupils replace Proper nouns with everyday pronouns.

Sheet 15 Once again the emphasis is on personal pronouns which are most appropriate at this level.

HALL OF MIRRORS

PAY HERE

Mark Sterling visited the Hall of Mirrors at the fair. Each mirror made him look different.

● Under each mirror write an adjective to describe how he looked.

tall _____ _____ _____ _____

● Draw other pictures on the back of this sheet.

● Ask a friend to write adjectives under them.

_____ _____ _____

PLANT TALK

Flora Bud needed new plants for her home. She described the kind of plant she wanted.

● Draw pictures of plants which fit Flora's descriptions.

climbing	spiky	bushy	flowering
budding	leafy	hanging	thorny

DESCRIBING ME

- Work in groups of 6 - 8 people.

- In your group ask the others to write one nice adjective about you in the space below. Each one should be different.

- Write at least 6 sentences about yourself.
  Each sentence should include one of the adjectives.

_____

_____

_____

_____

_____

_____

PHOTO

FIT

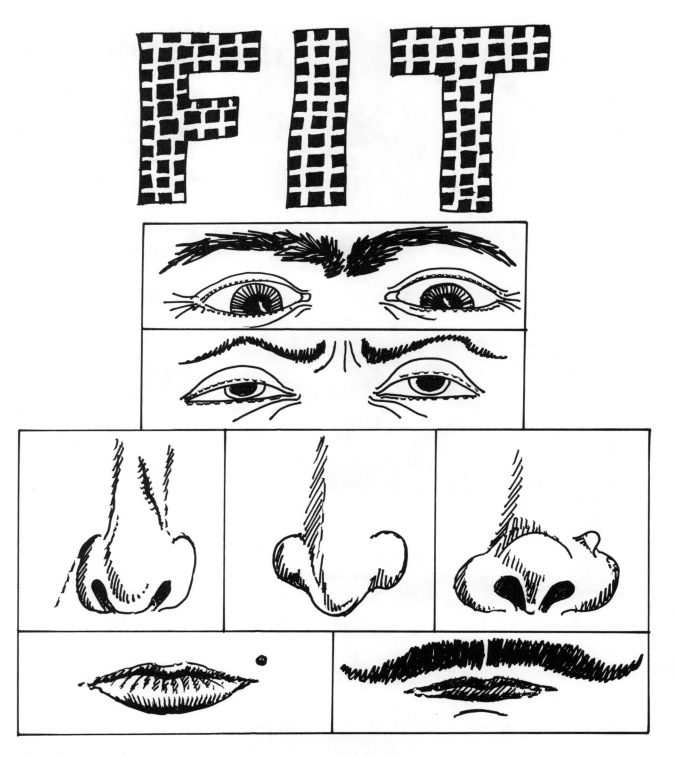

You have witnessed a crime.

- Choose the nose, eyes and mouth of the villain.

- Describe the villain accurately so that your partner will be able
  to cut out the correct parts and stick them on to the blank face.

_____   _____

_____   _____

MISCHIEF ZOO

ferocious

wriggly

striped

naughty

flying

talking

The monkeys have stolen the adjectives from the signs.

Do not walk across the _____ zebra.

Do not teach the _____ parrots rude words.

_____ snakes should not be used as scarves.

• Help the zookeeper by putting each adjective in the right place.

The _____ bats should not be used for cricket.

This cage is reserved for _____ children.

Heads put in the _____ lion's mouth cannot be replaced.

NAMING

Words which name are called **NOUNS.**

● Label the picture by writing the name in each box.

● Now sort your labels under three headings.

PEOPLE	PLACES	THINGS

IS IT PROPER?

Hi, I'm a boy. There are millions of boys so the word 'boy' is a **common** noun.

Hello, my name is Brian. There's only one of me so the word 'Brian' is a **proper** noun.

● Remember proper nouns always start with a capital letter.

● Make a list of proper nouns.

Name 10 places

Name 5 comics

● Make a list overleaf of:

10 people

5 roads

4 months

3 days

NAME THAT NOUN

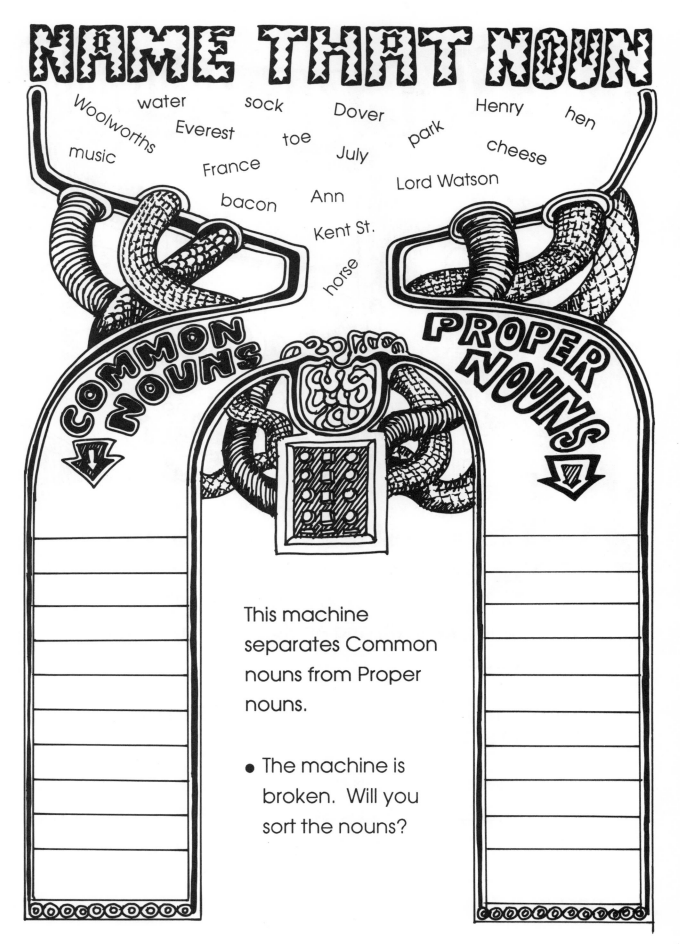

water   sock   Dover   Henry   hen

Woolworths   Everest   toe   July   park   cheese

music   France   bacon   Ann   Lord Watson

Kent St.

horse

COMMON NOUNS

PROPER NOUNS

This machine separates Common nouns from Proper nouns.

• The machine is broken. Will you sort the nouns?

HERE COME THE PRONOUNS

Let us into your sentences.

This is Kenneth. **Kenneth** is eight. **Kenneth's** sister is called Angie. **Angie** is very bossy. **Angie's** teacher complains that **Angie** talks too much. Kenneth and Angie play together. **Kenneth and Angie** are always playing tricks on people.

● REPLACE THE NOUNS IN BOLD WITH PRONOUNS TO MAKE THE TEXT READ BETTER.

This is Kenneth. _____ is eight. _____ sister is called Angie. _____ is very bossy. _____ teacher complains that _____ talks too much. Kenneth and Angie play together. _____ are always playing tricks on people.

I am a pronoun.
Use me and other
pronouns to write
about yourself.

_____ name is _____ .

_____ live at _____ .

_____ best friend is called _____ .

_____ is _____ years old.

_____ play together.

Sometimes _____ go to _____ houses.

Other times _____ comes to _____ .

- Use the pronouns on the ladder to complete the sentences.

- Write six sentences of your own using pronouns.

CAPITAL LETTERS AND FULL STOPS: SPEECH

Individual Masters

Capital Letters

Sheet 17 A simple introduction to the use of capitals for names. Discussion is valuable around the theme of capitals for both parts of a 'name' e.g. *Sleeping Beauty* or *Mr. Spock*. Children often use one capital but not two - in the belief that only the word 'Spock' is the name.

Sheets 18-19 Names remain the theme but we progress from people's names to the wider category of people and places. Sentences not beginning with a Proper noun have been given a capital letter so as not to point out that words such as Cardiff and Wales have a double entitlement in this passage.

Sheet 20 Adds to the third element of capital letters (i.e. beginning a sentence). In practice most pupils will have had considerable experience of this throughout Key Stage 1 but the sheet serves to reinforce the point that by learning new rules about capitals we don't forget the old ones!

Sheet 21 The sheet contains a number of contexual clues which you may wish to discuss with the children either before or after the exercise e.g. 'which words have capital letters? Which of them only have a capital if they start a sentence?'

Sheets 22-23 Contextual clues will help the children to categorise the 8 pieces into 4 beginnings and 4 ends. The map will help them to match beginnings and ends and to sequence the narrative.

Sheet 24 A straightforward piece of text which concentrates on bringing together the three uses of capital letters introduced earlier and at the same time reinforces full stops.

Sheet 25 This sheet will allow you to take an overview of whether or not the principles have been internalised and can transfer to pupils' own writing.

Speech

Sheet 26 The intention is to help pupils distinguish words actually spoken from the rest of the text. The task is a straightforward transfer of specific words from the base text to the illustrations.

Sheet 27 A reversal of the process in Sheet 26 designed to reinforce the idea.

Sheets 28-29 Now the pupil brings together words spoken and narrative to accompany the visuals. Support is provided in two of the pictures.

Sheets 30-31 No support is offered. The visuals and narrative are provided. The actual speech needs to be written by the child and it should take time, thought and a greater degree of precision in order to convey the exact meaning in the picture.
NB. The use of inverted commas is developed in the book **"Brain Waves Grammar For Upper Juniors"** which accompanies this volume.

Sheet 32 Here the pupil tells the story through dialogue. The writing reflects words actually spoken. The task of drawing their own picture sequence is important and should not be viewed as an optional extra.

Who goes there?

Titles and names

always start with a capital

letter → **Mrs.** **Brown.**

Match the names to the pictures.
Use capital letters for names and titles.

rapunzel	sleeping beauty	doctor who
mr. moon	captain hook	tom thumb
peter pan	mr. spock	miss muffet

Me and my world

My name is linford thompson.
My house is called greyfriars.
greyfriars is in station road. station
road is in cardiff. cardiff is a city
in wales. wales is part of the united
kingdom. The united kingdom is a country in
europe. europe is one of the continents in the world.

Match the correct sentence to each picture.
Use capital letters for the names of people and places.

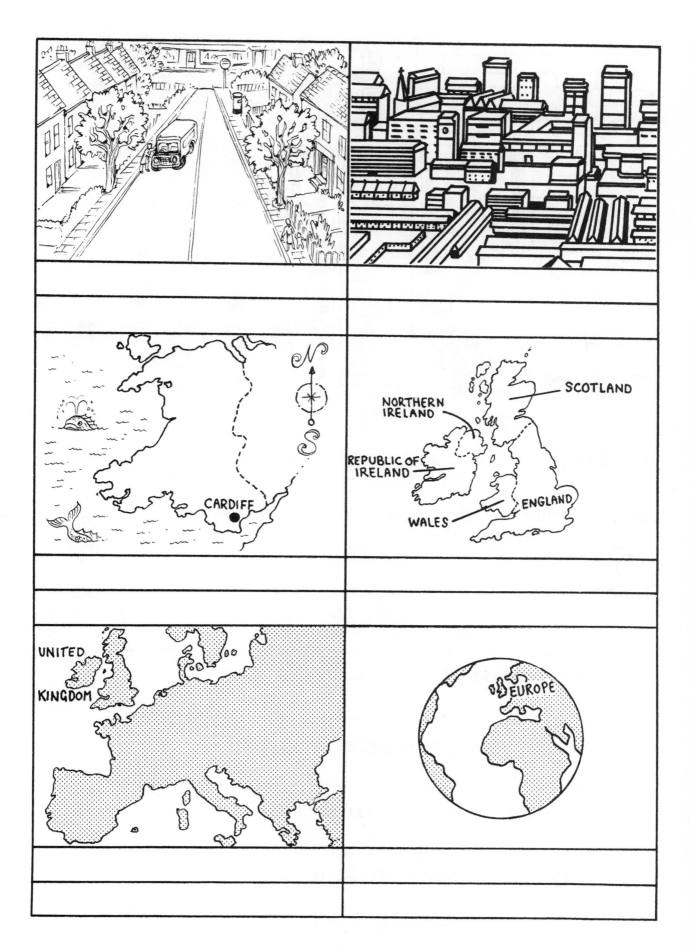

CAPITAL LETTERS

Names of people, places and when starting sentences.

"If I'm chosen to start a sentence, a name or a place I can look like you."

Write the sentence putting capital letters in the right place.

1. i went to london with my friend nina.

_____

2. we travelled by bus to buckingham palace.

_____

3. nina was hoping to see prince harry.

_____

4. the queen drove past in a rolls royce.

_____

5. we finished the day at the tower of london

_____

YOU SHOULD HAVE 16 CAPITAL LETTERS.

SUPER STOP

Enid has a problem.

No-one can understand her story because she never ends her sentences properly.

Where should Super Stop make his mark?

The giant crept up behind me I was

scared stiff I could feel his breath on

the back of my neck I decided to

make a run for it He chased

me along High Street and into

the shop I rushed to the

checkout and

CORRECT AND FINISH ENID'S STORY.

Lost Treasure

Captain Eggwhisk was the most dangerous pirate in the seven seas. Along with his cut throat pirates he buried treasure on Dead Eye Island. The treasure map directions were cut into 8 pieces. Each pirate took one piece.

Walk along the path

Go across the

Stop under the

past the swamp

the pine wood

Run through

oak tree

stepping stones

Cut out the directions and make four full sentences.
Now look at the treasure map.

Dead Eye Island

Treasure Hunt

X START

White Ridge Hills

Sink Swamp

Claret Cave

Put your sentences in the correct order.

Stick them down.

Mark where the treasure is buried.

START AND STOP

A sentence starts with a capital letter and ends with a .

Write out the story correctly.

duke william sailed to england in the year 1066 he brought an army with him william knew he would have to fight against harold the leader of the saxons the fighting lasted all day harold was killed by an arrow and duke william's army won the battle and william became king of england

Write at least four sentences about the picture.

_____

_____

_____

_____

_____

_____

_____

What a drip

- Look at the picture sequence and read the text.

- Write into the speech bubbles only the words which are spoken.

- Think of another nursery rhyme and draw a picture sequence.
  Do this on the back of this sheet.

- Add speech bubbles and text.

Dr. Foster waved goodbye to his wife and said, " I'm going to Gloucester."

Dr. Foster called, " Good morning" to his neighbour, Mr. Fish. Mr Fish replied, " Looks like rain to me."

Mr Fish was right, it poured down.
Dr. Foster stepped in a puddle and cried out, "Oh no! It's up to my middle."

Dr. Foster turned for home and muttered, "I'll never go there again."

Feeling Sheepish

- Look at the picture sequence and read the text.

- Write in the text the words that are spoken.

- Choose another nursery rhyme and do the same with it on the other side of this sheet.

Farmer Trotter was surprised when he entered the kitchen. He shouted,"____ ____ ____ ____ ____ ? "

Farmer Trotter was angry. He called, "____ ____ ____ ____ ____ ____ ____ ____ ?"

He was hopping mad when the sheep answered, "____ ____ ____ ____ ____ ____ ____ ."

When Farmer Trotter found Boy Blue, he roared, "____ ____ ____ ____ ____ ____ ____ ____ ."

- You need to know the story of Red Riding Hood.

- Look at the picture sequence.

- Complete the speech bubbles.

- Under each picture write a caption which tells the story.

"Keep to the path, there is a wolf in the forest."

Red Riding Hood's Grandma was ill. Red Riding Hood set off to visit her.

The wolf jumped out from behind a tree.

"Grandma it's only me, can I come in?"

THERE'S A WOLF ABOUT!

OVER THE

- Read the narrative.

- Write in the speech bubbles what you think the characters said.

Carl and Lisa were bird watching on the coast. Carl leaned over the cliff edge. Lisa warned him to be careful but Carl ignored her. He was in search of a rare gull's nest.

Carl became excited when he spotted the eggs. He turned to tell Lisa what he had found but lost his footing and fell. Lisa heard Carl scream as he disappeared from sight.

Lisa could not believe it. She rushed to the cliff edge and was relieved to find that Carl had fallen on to a ledge. She stretched out her arm and tried in vain to reach him.

Lisa knew she would need to find help before dark. Carl did not want to be left but realised that Lisa was right. Lisa kept her head and acted quickly.

Lisa ran faster than she had ever run before. She shouted at the top of her voice as she approached the nearest farm house.

She explained the situation breathlessly. The farmer lost no time, the Land Rover was soon speeding towards Carl - but the weather was growing misty as night approached.

The farmer attached one end of his rope to the Land Rover. He gave Carl clear instructions. Within minutes Carl was safe.

Everyone was relieved but the farmer was angry that they had foolishly risked their lives.

- The pictures tell a story.

- In the speech bubbles write what you think each person says.

- Compare your sheet with a friend.

- Draw a sequence of pictures to tell a story.

- Ask a friend to fill in the speech bubbles.

QUESTIONS: APOSTROPHES: EXCLAMATIONS

Questions

Sheet 34 The answers provide clues to the questions. The Snow White theme allows pupils to draw on their knowledge of the story.

Sheet 35 Extends the task. Now the children must construct their own questions but they need to frame them in the light of their choice of an interviewee. Useful discussion can precede the choice. Certain 'famous people' are likely to appeal to some children more than others. You will need to decide whether or not the interviewee should be a real person and/or still alive.

Sheet 36 Here the child distinguishes between questions and statements.

Sheet 37 Another matching exercise. Not all questions expect or require answers but in this section we have focused on questions which do.

Apostrophes

The apostrophe is often misplaced, not only in pupils' writing but also in that of many adults. We deal with the possession aspect of the use of the apostrophe in the book **"Brain Waves Grammar For Upper Juniors"**. In this book we concentrate on the apostrophe as used to indicate missing letter(s).

Sheet 38 A simple introduction which shows a space where the missing letter could be. The pupil first marks the space with an apostrophe as in the example and then writes the words in full. Useful discussion can centre around verbal as distinct from written English. If the children analyse their spoken vocabulary they can compare it with *a)* novels they are reading, and *b)* formal grammar books they may use.

Sheet 39 Reverses the process of Sheet 38 by moving from the full form to the shortened form.

Exclamations

These express the degree to which a speaker is moved by something. They can be found in sentence form but at this level we have concentrated on single words or short phrases which reflect the most common usage.

Sheet 40 A straightforward classification into exclamation and non-exclamation is all that is asked for but you may wish to further categorise the non-exclamation sentences.

Sheet 41 This time the pupils must think of their own words and select those which match the action and would be followed by an exclamation mark.

MISSING GIRL FOUND

World exclusive by The Young Reporter
of the Year.   Ida Story.

Write the questions Ida asked.

Today I interviewed a runaway princess. I asked her questions. These are her answers.

_____ • My name is Snow White.

_____ • I lived in a castle with my
_____   father and stepmother.

_____ • I think she was jealous of me.

_____ • She told a huntsman to kill me.

_____ • I suppose he felt sorry
_____   for me.

_____ • I just wandered through the
_____   forest until I found a small
_____   cottage.

_____ • No I'm not afraid, there are
_____   seven other people
_____   living there.

_____ • She might try to kill me.

_____

THE YOUNG REPORTER OF THE YEAR

You have the chance to interview a famous person.

• Draw a picture of the person.

• Write an interesting headline above the picture.

• Write a caption below the picture.

• Draft 12 questions you will ask in the interview.

QUESTIONS _____

_____

_____

_____

_____

_____

_____ CONTINUE OVERLEAF ▶

ASKING QUESTIONS

- Decide which of these sentences are questions.

- Put a question mark at the end of each question.

- Put a full stop at the end of the others.

QUESTIONS AND ANSWERS

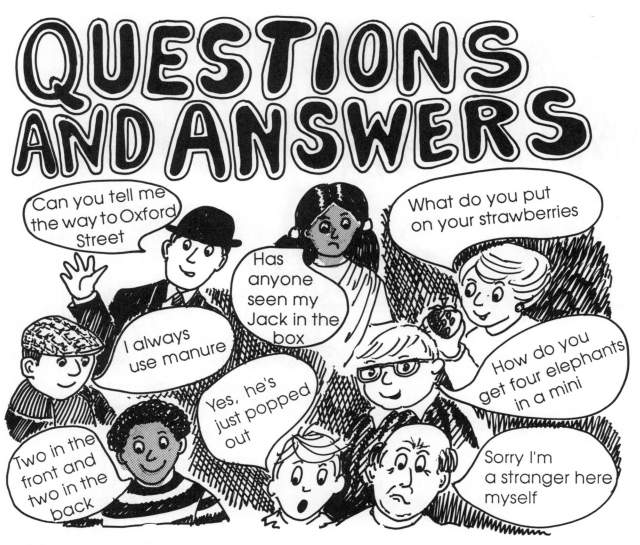

- Match the answers to the questions.

- Remember to add question marks.

QUESTIONS

1 _____

_____

2 _____

_____

3 _____

_____

4 _____

ANSWERS

1 _____

_____

2 _____

_____

3 _____

_____

4 _____

The case of the Missing Letters

Letters have been missed out
of these words.

● Help Sherlock by marking with
an apostrophe where the letter
is missing.

The first one is done for you.

don't ⟶ do not

doesn't ⟶

Ill ⟶

whats ⟶

Im ⟶

shes ⟶

cant ⟶

● Write the matching word.

● How many more can you think of?

AMAR'S DIARY

Amar keeps his diary on a computer disc. Read what he typed in.

I do not know why I have been sent to my room. I cannot say sorry for something that was not my fault. What is the point of being given a bike if I am not allowed to swop it for an old fishing rod? If they could not trust me they should not have given it to me. I blame George. He is the one. I will never speak to him again. He will be sorry. It does not bother me that we shall not be friends.

● Write out Amar's diary using shorthand forms.

● Use apostrophes to mark the missing letters.

_____

_____

_____

_____

_____

_____

_____

_____

_____

SPLASH

- Exclamation marks usually follow a shout or a surprise.

- Some of the speech bubbles need exclamation marks.

Happy Birthday

- Fill in the speech bubbles.

- Use exclamation marks in six of the bubbles.

- Write sentences which do not need exclamation marks in the other four.

Gender

Sheet 43 Some discussion of appropriate vocabulary may be needed here. Pupils may be able to determine the meaning of masculine/feminine/male/female from the examples if they do not know the vocabulary.

Sheet 44 Other pairs of words can be drawn from the children's own interest and knowledge.

Tenses

There is no true future tense in English, we normally add will/shall to form the future.

Sheet 45 A basic classification exercise. Discussion should centre around the key words that give us clues about whether words are Past, Present or Future.

Sheet 46 The same actions are now placed in the three tenses. The lack of a true future tense can be discussed here. As can the variety of forms in which the past tense can be written.

Singular/Plural

Sheet 47 We introduce the words singular/plural quite consciously. It is valuable if pupils are exposed to this kind of specific vocabulary early and are then encouraged to make use of such language.

Sheet 48 Moves on from simply recognising nouns in singular or plural form to exploring the need for agreement between the noun and its verb. This does not require sentence analysis skills but should be based on what pupils hear, understand and in many cases say in their everyday lives.

Duck here comes the DRAKE

Feminine means female.
Masculine means male.

"The lioness does all the killing. I like to look my best."

Feminine	Masculine
Lioness Duck	Lion Drake

● Complete the chart.

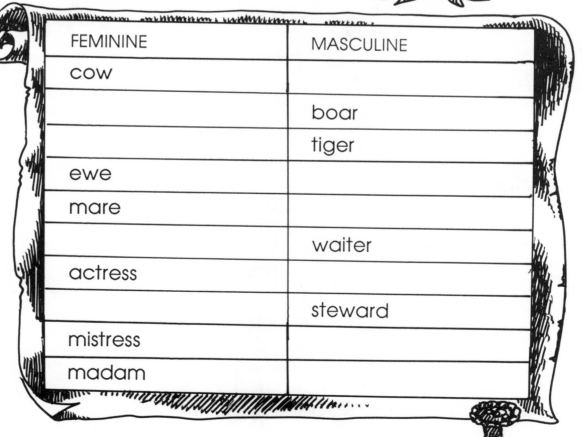

FEMININE	MASCULINE
cow	
	boar
	tiger
ewe	
mare	
	waiter
actress	
	steward
mistress	
madam	

● How many more pairs of masculine and feminine words can you think of?

MALE OR FEMALE?

● Some words are
used only for males
and others for females.

● Complete the pairs
of words.

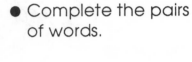

Prince	Princess
King	_____
_____	Mrs.
Brother	_____
_____	Aunt
Grandad	_____
_____	Niece
Son	_____
_____	Mother
Duke	_____
_____	Countess

SCHOOL LIFE

• Fill in the gaps so that each sentence is written in the past, present and future.

YESTERDAY	TODAY	TOMORROW
Mr. Sloan marked the register.	Mr. Sloan marks the register.	Mr. Sloan will mark the register.
	The class goes to the swimming baths.	
We ran to catch the school bus.		
	We play rounders at break time.	The cook will make ravioli for dinner.
I was in trouble for laughing in class.		
		We shall try harder.

● Sort the words into two sets.

Words which mean one.

Words which mean more than one.

horse	person	children	coats
men	elephants	carpet	glove
shoe	women	bicycle	handbag

ONE	MORE THAN ONE

● A noun which means only one object is SINGULAR in number.

● A noun which means more than one object is PLURAL in number.

SINGULAR AND PLURAL

- Write two sentences for each of the nouns.
  One in its singular form.
  One in its plural form.
  The first is done for you.

toe	mice	gloves
children	drawer	parcel
summer	friend	eggs
year	tomatoes	sister

SINGULAR	PLURAL
My toe was hurting.	My toes were hurting.